1. How do we explore the past?

The people in this photograph are carefully uncovering the remains of a Roman villa.

▲ **1.** Find out what a Roman villa was. Draw a picture and write a few sentences to describe it.

This Roman villa was first discovered in 1864 by a gamekeeper. There are still parts of it to be uncovered. The people are making an exact record of what they find and where they found it.

● **A.** What is a gamekeeper? Look it up in a dictionary.

The photograph above shows a man "brass-rubbing" in a church. Brasses mark where important people are buried. By making rubbings, we can look at the armour and the clothes worn by people long ago.

● **B.** Brasses also act as memorials to people. Look up memorial in a dictionary.
● **C.** Why do you think important memorials were made in brass? Iron was cheaper. Why was this not used? (What happens to iron after a long time?)
● **D.** Why do these people want to explore the past?

1

2. Historical objects

As we walk through our home town or village, we often do not notice objects which tell us something about the past. As we travel around, especially by car, we miss many interesting things. For example, thousands of holiday-makers travel to the south coast in summer. Most of them do not notice unusual milestones like the one in the photograph. They are found on the A22 between Eastbourne and East Grinstead.

The figures on the milestone tell us how many miles we are from London. In the past, many people could not read, so it would be no use writing "London" on the milestone. Instead, there was a picture of a bell with a bow. Bow Church (Bow Bells) is in the centre of the city of London.

There is also a buckle on the stone. It is called the "Pelham" buckle. It told travellers that they were crossing land owned by Lord Pelham.

● **A.** How could people tell that they were 54 miles from London by looking at the milestone?

A class in a school in Tewkesbury thought that they would like to look at interesting objects from the past in their district. Many of the towns near Tewkesbury such as Worcester are famous for their historic buildings. The class decided to go out into the country and search for things that are less well-known than these buildings. They kept to within about 16 kilometres of Tewkesbury.

The class was divided into groups. Each group was given a part of the surrounding area to study. They kept a log book of what they found. Many of the class lived in the villages and looked at places near their home after school.

VILLAGE LOG BOOK				
WORK GROUP C.		LEADER C. Wilkins		DIRECTION East
DATE Friday 12th May				FROM TEWKESBURY
VILLAGE	ROAD DISTANCE FROM TEWKESBURY	OBJECT	LOCATION	NOTES
BREDON	3 miles	Tithe Barn	In farmyard at end of village	National Trust collection box on wall
		Direction post Almshouses Prehistoric hill fort	alongside main road near centre of village on top of hill	
KEMERTON	3¾ miles	Nothing		
OVERBURY	4½ miles	Lychgate	In front of Church	memorial inside (very pretty village)
CONDERTON	5 miles	Prehistoric hill fort ('Dane's Camp)	1½ miles from village on hill	
ASHTON UNDER THE HILL	10 miles	village cross with sundial on top	In front of Church by crossroads	
KERSOE	11½ miles	nothing		
ELMLEY CASTLE	13 miles	Queen Elizabeth Inn Sundial Village cross	High Street near Church In Churchyard Bottom end of High St.	Queen Elizabeth visited village

Here is a page of the logbook belonging to Group C. Their teacher helped them to set it out.

● **B.** How can you tell that all the villages were visited on the same day?

● **C.** How many villages had sundials?

● **D.** The group liked the look of Overbury village. How can you tell from the log book? Did they need to add the extra comment?

● **E.** Did they also record something extra about Elmley Castle?
If so, what?

▲ **1.** Find out something about the following objects that Group C found.
hill forts
sundials
lych gates
You could use a dictionary or a book from the library.

3

Making a map

When the groups had finished their work, they made a map like the one on page 5. It showed where they had found objects that interested them. Under the map they put a key to show what the symbols on the map stood for.

Look at the map and answer these questions.

● **A.** How many tithe barns did the class find?
● **B.** In which village did they find the most historical objects?
● **C.** How many towns shown on the map lie on the river Severn? Name them.
● **D.** What two objects were found at Forthampton?
● **E.** Why do you think these objects were side by side?
● **F.** Which villages have mills?
● **G.** Why do you think the mills were built?

▲ **1.** Find Tewkesbury in an atlas.

The class put the photographs they had taken on the wall round the map so that everyone could see what they looked like. The one which interested people most was the photograph of the whipping post at Forthampton.

The whipping post at Forthampton.

▲ **2.** You have been placed in the stocks for a day. Write or tape sentences about how you feel. What did people who saw you say and do?

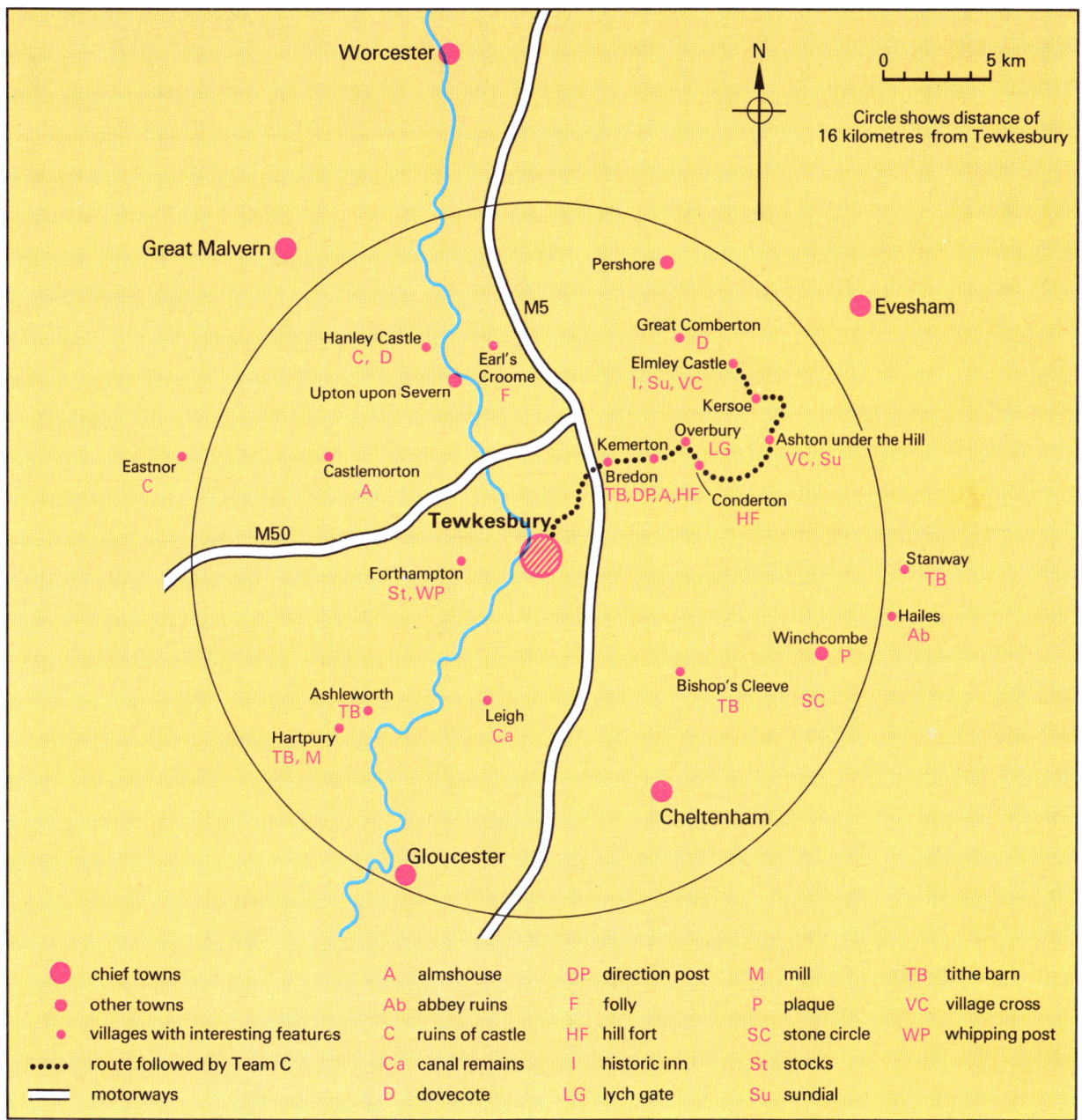

N

0   5 km

Circle shows distance of
16 kilometres from Tewkesbury

Worcester

Great Malvern

Pershore

Evesham

M5

Hanley Castle
C, D

Earl's
Croome
F

Upton upon Severn

Great Comberton
D

Elmley Castle
I, Su, VC

Kersoe

Eastnor
C

Castlemorton
A

Kemerton

Overbury
LG

Ashton under the Hill
VC, Su

Bredon
TB, DP, A, HF

Conderton
HF

M50

Tewkesbury

Stanway
TB

Forthampton
St, WP

Hailes
Ab

Winchcombe
P

Ashleworth
TB

Leigh
Ca

Bishop's Cleeve
TB

SC

Hartpury
TB, M

Cheltenham

Gloucester

●	chief towns	A	almshouse	DP	direction post	M	mill	TB tithe barn
●	other towns	Ab	abbey ruins	F	folly	P	plaque	VC village cross
•	villages with interesting features	C	ruins of castle	HF	hill fort	SC	stone circle	WP whipping post
•••••	route followed by Team C	Ca	canal remains	I	historic inn	St	stocks	
—	motorways	D	dovecote	LG	lych gate	Su	sundial	

5

A history dictionary

Some members of the class did not know what all of the objects were. So the class made their history dictionary. Here are some of the explanations.

Almshouses Rich people gave money so that houses could be built in the village for poor people. This was often the only help that poor people in the past could have.

Dovecot In the Middle Ages animals could not be kept in the winter. So they were killed in the autumn. Important people kept doves in dovecots so they would have fresh meat for the winter. Ordinary people were not allowed to do this because doves ate the corn in the fields.

Folly Rich people sometimes built things which were nice to look at, but had no use. This was fashionable about 100 years ago. Often, a folly would look like the ruins of an old castle.

Almshouses at Chipping Campden in Gloucestershire.

Hill fort Before the Romans came to Britain, other warlike people had arrived here. To be safe from attack, they built villages on hill tops. They made banks, ditches and high fences called stockades around the villages. We can still see the banks and ditches today.

Plaque A tablet on a wall. It has been put up as a memorial to somebody or something.

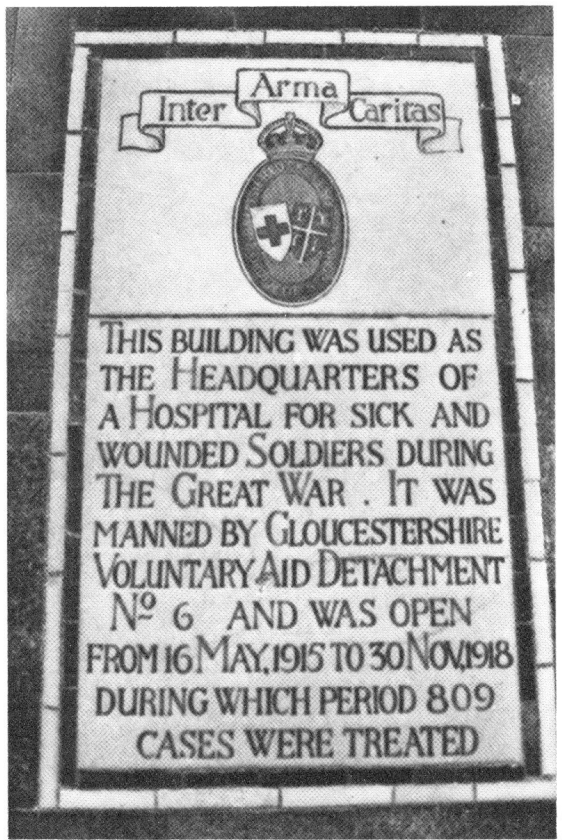

Tithe barn In the past, farmers had to pay a tax (tithe) to the Church. Often the tithe was crops, such as hay or wheat. These were sometimes stored in the tithe barns owned by large churches and abbeys.

▲ **1.** Look again at the map and the symbols beneath it on page 5. Write down the words that you would put in the dictionary.

● **A.** Why are the words the class wrote down in this order?
● **B.** There are not many almshouses now. Why is this?
● **C.** Which definition does the picture on the left show?

7

3. Oral history

Oral history is history that we can learn from talking to older people. They can remember important events which happened in the past.

▲ **1.** Count how many people in your class were born in the village or town in which they live today.

Many people move away from their home districts to find work. In some jobs people are expected to move home quite often. Many children have grandparents who live in a different part of the country.

● **A.** Think of jobs in which people are expected to move home several times.
● **B.** Why do some people feel homesick when they first leave home?

In some parts of Britain there are still villages which have few new people coming to live in them. The village in the photograph is one of them. It is a mining village in South Wales. It is called Bedlinog.

▲ **2.** Find South Wales in your atlas. You will not find Bedlinog marked, but you will find

the nearby town of Merthyr Tydfil. It lies to the north of Cardiff.

● **C.** Look at the photograph of Bedlinog. How can you tell that this is a village and not a town?
● **D.** Why do you think some old people find it hard to live there?
● **E.** Does anything in the picture help to show that Bedlinog is in South Wales? (*Clue*, what sort of countryside is it?)

Many people have moved away from Bedlinog to find work, but very few people have moved into it. Apart from the coal mine and a few shops, there is no other work in the village. The houses are small and old. Some people have moved away to buy better houses.

In one class in the village school, 21 out of 28 children were born in the village. Fifteen of the children have grandparents living there.

Many of the miners' families in Bedlinog still live in small cottages like these.

▲ **2.** Draw a bar chart to show the number of children in the class in Bedlinog. Draw another bar to show the number with grandparents living in the village.

The class decided that they would like to explore the history of their village. The teacher asked all of them to do two things:

1. To choose something that interested them.
2. To talk to elderly people in the village about that topic.

One of the boys chose transport as his topic. He went to see his father's uncle to talk about it. The old man had been a miner until he retired.

The man asked "What do you mean by 'transport'?"
"Things that carry us from one place to another like a train or a bus," answered the boy.

● **D.** What other examples could the boy have used to explain the word "transport"?

The boy took a tape recorder with him to record their talk. He had to visit the old man more than once because the old man had so much to tell him.

9

Later, the boy wrote out some of the more interesting things he had learned about transport in the village in the past. The rest of the class were then able to read what he had discovered.

Here are the sixteen things he wrote:

1. The village was not easy to get to, the old ways of getting from place to place were still used here.

The farmers used "carts" without wheels to bring hay or dried bracken from the steep hillsides to the farms. The bracken was used for winter bedding for the animals.

2. The farms were small and the land was poor quality. So most farmers only had one working horse. At harvest time they had to help each other to harvest the hay and the oats. They borrowed each others' horses to pull large carts called "gambos".

3. Horses were also used in the coal mines. "Pit ponies" were used underground to pull small iron waggons called "trams".

Shire horses were used to move heavy loads and equipment in the mines. Some of them worked on the surface of the mine which was called "top pit". The best working horses were groomed and decorated to take part in local horse shows.

● **A.** What is bracken? Why did farmers use it for bedding for the animals?
● **B.** Why were pit ponies used down in the pits (mines), and not the stronger shire horses?

4. In the village, the big horses from the pit were used to deliver one ton loads of coal to the houses.

A miner having his back scrubbed.

10

5. Cheap coal was given to the miners as part of their wages. Most of the houses were in terraces and the coal was often dumped in front of the house.

The miner was usually at work, so his wife often had to carry the coal right through the house in buckets to the coalhouse in the back yard. It was a filthy job, and the house had to be scrubbed afterwards.

The coal was needed for the large coal fires which kept the stone-built house warm. The fire also heated the oven for baking. Wives heated buckets of water on the fire every afternoon so that the men could have a hot bath when they came home from the pit.

● C. What is a "terrace"?
● D. Why was coal dumped on the pavement?
● E. Why did the men have a bath at home? Where do today's miners wash after work?

▲ 1. You have read that miners get cheap coal as part of their wages. Make a list of other jobs in which people are given special prices or advantages called 'perks'. Here are some jobs to start with.
Teachers get long holidays.
Bank managers get cheap loans to buy houses.

Horses being led away from the mines after a day's work.

6. Children in the village saw the pit ponies in the field behind the school. The ponies were brought to the surface once a year for a rest. After working in the dark and living in underground stables, they were blind when they came out of the pit.

▲ 2. You are a miner or a miner's wife in the past. Write down or tape the things you dislike most about your life.

11

8. Getting up was a problem. To make sure that they would get up in time to catch the train, some workmen paid a friend (a "butty") to knock them up. He would tap a split bamboo cane or a thin stick against the bedroom window. He could also whistle a signal which the man in bed would recognise.

● **B.** Why didn't the butty shout to wake up his friend?

9. On Whit Saturday, a special train left the village to take the miners and their families on a Sunday School trip to the seaside. They usually went to Barry Island. The children were given some pocket money by the Chapel they went to on Sundays.

● **C.** When is Whit Sunday? Why was it a good day for the Sunday School trip?

7. When the pits in the village were first opened, men and boys from other places travelled to work in them. They came by train in special wooden carriages. The carriages were like cattle trucks. They had wooden seats. One of the two trains that ran each day was called "The Squib". To get to work on time some of the men had to catch a train at 4.40 a.m.

● **A.** Why were the workmen's trains so uncomfortable?

10. Some of the pits could not be reached by train. The men who worked in these pits had to walk to work down the valley or over the hills to neighbouring valleys. Some men walked five miles to work and cut coal with a pick all day. Then they had to walk home, tired and dirty, often in the rain.

▲ **1.** What does a pick look like? Draw a picture or describe it on tape.

Some of the Bedlinog miners used to travel to this mine.

The "Lady Aberfan" looked like this London bus.

Here is what the old miner said:
"I walked back and forth to the pit for five years. Walking in wet clothes, I couldn't turn back because I needed the money. Only £2.10s.0d. a week I earned and you know I had a family.

▲ **2.** Write £2.10s.0d. in today's money.

11. Bus services began in the area about 1928 (he was not sure of the date). The first bus took people five miles down the valley to catch another bus or a train to nearby towns. The bus was an old London double-decker bus like the one in the picture. The upstairs seats had been taken out.

The bus was called the "Lady Aberfan", because the owner lived in the village of Aberfan. The conductor was a local man and he decided on the spot whether to charge you 1, 2 or 3 pennies for the fare. This service was replaced by a better service to the town of Merthyr. This bus was called the "Bedlinog Queen".

13

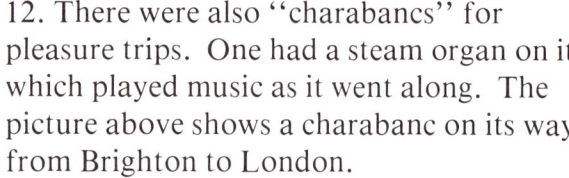

12. There were also "charabancs" for pleasure trips. One had a steam organ on it which played music as it went along. The picture above shows a charabanc on its way from Brighton to London.

13. Because miners travelled home from work covered in coal dust, they did not travel on the normal bus service. Some of them went to work in an old furniture van fitted with wooden seats. Later, there was a regular workmen's bus service to and from the pit.

● **A.** What are two advantages of having a special workmen's bus service to the pit?

14. In 1948 the winter was very hard. Heavy falls of snow blocked the railway and the roads. Some of the younger miners slid down the hill from their homes on their metal food boxes. Then they walked along the valley to the pit.

15. The railway station closed in 1961. The railway is still used to carry coal away from the mine.

16. In the past, most families were poor, so very few could afford a car. The very first car in the village belonged to the family of a grocer who was better off than the miners. Today, most miners travel to work in their own cars.

The first car in the village of Bedlinog was the same kind as this one.

● **B.** Why is it better to carry coal by train rather than by road?

● **C.** Why do you think the grocer was better off than the miners?

▲ **1.** Choose one of the following topics. Write or tape a short story about it.

    Working with pit ponies
    The winter of 1948
    A ride in a charabanc
    A trip to the seaside

Remember that this account of transport in the past comes from one old man. He may not have been correct in everything he said, though he had a very good memory for all kinds of things.

Checking facts

How can we check that what he told us was true?

We could ask other people in the village questions about what he had said. If they gave the same answer as he had, we would be more certain of the facts.

We could also go to the library in the nearby town and ask to see old copies of the local newspaper. Some events would have been headline news — the winter of 1948, for example.

In this way, we can build up a clear and correct picture of the past.

15

4. Town trails

Many of our historic towns have so many ancient churches, historic buildings and memorials that it is difficult to find what you want to see. Some of the streets are narrow and twisting, so it is easy to get lost.

Many visitors are only able to spend a little time in the town. If they do not know their way round, they may miss the most interesting sights. One way of solving this problem is to make a town trail. A town trail is a path or track through the town. It is planned to make sure that you see what you want to see as you walk along.

How to make a town trail

We shall look at a town trail which some students made for Monmouth in Gwent.

Monmouth is an old-fashioned market town. It lies on the A40, a main road from London to South Wales. It is close to the Wye valley, a famous holiday area. Nearby are the remains of castles such as Raglan, and churches such as Tintern Abbey. Many tourists visit Monmouth because it is near such interesting places. Most people can only spend an hour or two in the town.

▲ **1.** Use an atlas to find Monmouth. Draw a sketch map to show its position. Make sure you include the River Wye. Add places of interest to tourists, for example, Tintern Abbey, Raglan Castle. You can find other places to add to your map by looking at library books and tourist guides.

Here is how the students made a town trail of Monmouth.

A view of Monmouth.

16

1. They bought the official town guide. In the guide there was a town plan. There was also some information about the main places of interest in the town.

2. The students made a list of the most important places named in the guide book.

3. They then visited each of the places on the list to see how interesting it was.

   At each place they made notes of what could be seen there. They took photographs or made sketches of the best places or objects.

4. The students also visited old parts of the town which the guide book did not mention, to see if there were other places or objects to add to the list. They took photographs of these too.

   One building not included in the guide book was the famous public school, Monmouth School.

5. Since many of the visitors to Monmouth do not stay long, the students decided that the trail should allow visitors to see the most important things in less than two hours. If they were in a hurry, they could leave out the museum. Then the trail would only take about one hour.

St Peter's Church, Dixton.

6. So the students had to leave out some of the places listed. St. Peter's Church, Dixton, had to be left out, although many visitors would be very interested in it.

● **A.** Why was it useful to buy a town guide to help to make the town trail?

● **B.** Why was it sensible to make a trail which took less than two hours to go round?

● **C.** Look at the map on page 18. Why did the students leave St. Peter's Church, Dixton, off their town trail?

17

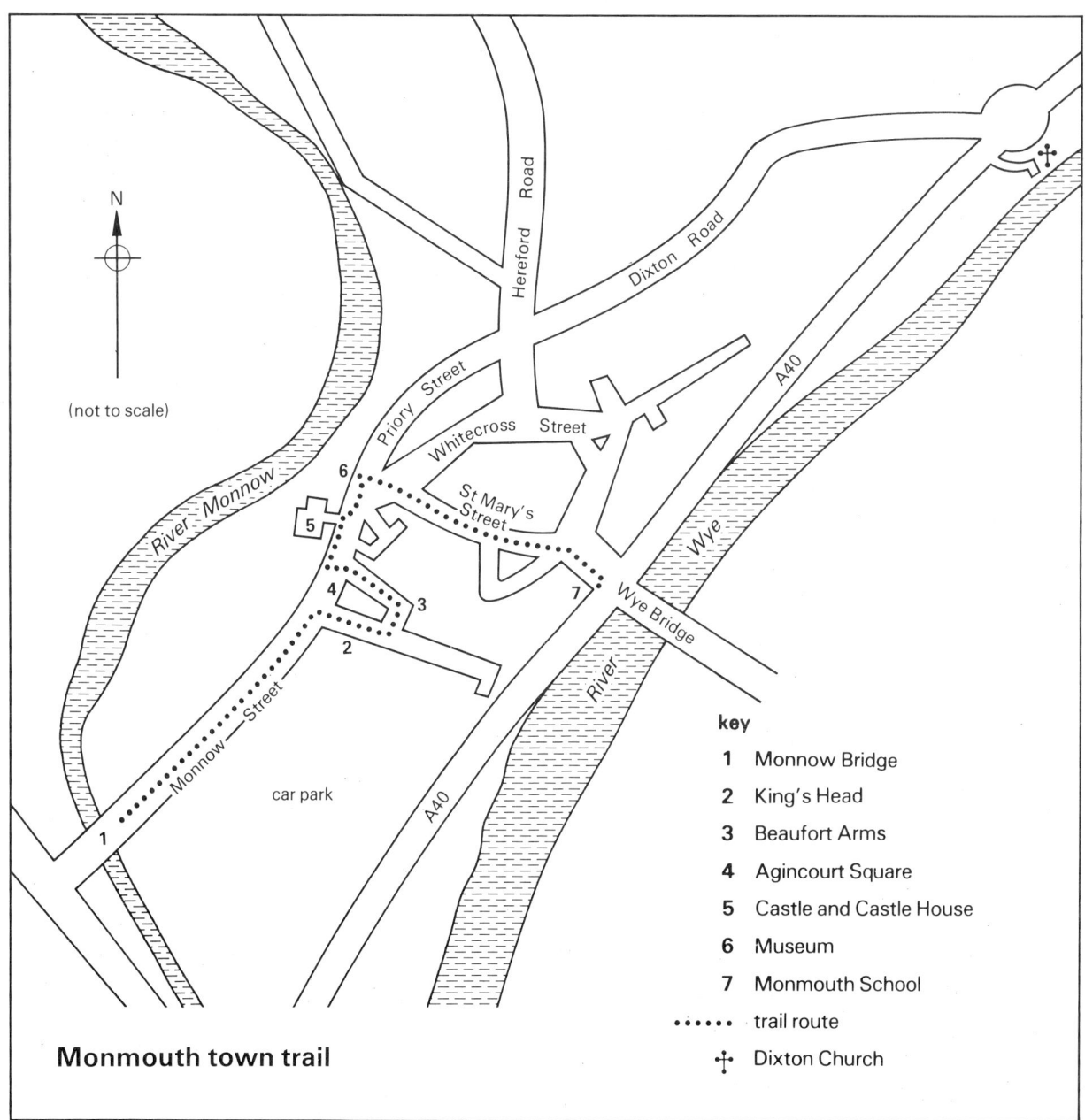

key
1 Monnow Bridge
2 King's Head
3 Beaufort Arms
4 Agincourt Square
5 Castle and Castle House
6 Museum
7 Monmouth School
•••••• trail route
✝ Dixton Church

Monmouth town trail

A town trail in Monmouth

Start

Leave main car park through market. Turn left in Monnow St. to the Monnow Bridge.

1. Monnow Bridge

This is the only fortified bridge left in Britain. It was built in the 13th century. It has been a guardhouse, prison and watchtower. Monmouth once had 4 gates and a town wall. The gate is now a traffic bottleneck, and the A40 by-passes the town centre (see map).

Follow Monnow St. towards town centre. Notice the Vine Tree Inn on right — 17th century. Note the ancient doorway. At the end of street turn right.

2. King's Head

A 17th century coaching inn. Coaches left the King's Head twice a day for London. Named after King Henry V but often visited by Charles I. There is a figure of King Charles in the bar.

4. Agincourt Square
Named after the famous victory of Henry V. He was born in Monmouth Castle. On the front of the Shire Hall, there is a statue of him. In front of Shire Hall there is also a statue of C.S. Rolls of Rolls-Royce holding an aeroplane. He was the son of Lord Llangattock, a local landowner.

Go round to the front of Shire Hall and into Agincourt Square.

Go around block behind Shire Hall.

3. Beaufort Arms
Another old coaching inn with rival services to London. Coaches to Bristol, Brecon and Cheltenham stopped here. On the doors there is the portcullis badge of the Tudors and the House of Commons. Nelson slept here when he visited Monmouth.

With Shire Hall at your back, cross the road and turn to the right. Then take the first turn to the left.

Return to the main street and turn left along Priory St. This street was built on the site of the old Bullring. Just beyond Woolworth's is the old market hall which contains the museum.

5. Castle and Castle House

The castle was built about 1068 and was destroyed by the Parliamentarians in the Civil War. Henry V was born there in 1387. Castle House was later built on the ruins (1673). It is now the headquarters of the Royal Monmouthshire Royal Engineers.

21

6. Museum — Local History Centre and Nelson Museum

The local history centre contains interesting relics of shipping on the River Wye. It also has a display on crime and punishment in the past, and on farming. It contains a 'Monmouth Cap'. In a Shakespeare play a man called Fluellen speaks of men 'wearing leeks in the Monmouth caps'. The Nelson museum contains all kinds of things connected with this hero.

On coming out of the museum, cross the road and follow St. Mary's St. to the Wye Bridge. From the bridge you can look back at the school.

7. Monmouth School

Founded in 1614 in the reign of James I. It was founded by a local man who had made his fortune as a haberdasher in London. (A haberdasher is a person who sells things like ribbons and thread.) This is a boys' school but there is also a Monmouth School for girls.

RETURN TO CAR PARK

THE END!

22

Look at the town trail of Monmouth and answer these questions.

- **A.** Why was a fortified bridge put on the gate?
- **B.** What problem does the fortified gate cause today?
- **C.** Why were some inns called coaching inns?
- **D.** Why do you think that the statue of C.S. Rolls shows him holding an aeroplane?
- **E.** What other object might C.S. Rolls have been shown with?
- **F.** Who was the leader of the Parliamentarians in the Civil War?
- **G.** What was another name for the Parliamentarians?
- **H.** What do we mean when we say that he "founded a school"?

▲ **1.** Here is a list of some of the historical events you have read about in this chapter. You are also given the dates when they happened. Put them in the correct historical order (the oldest first).

    The building of Monmouth Castle (1068)
    The birth of Henry V (1387)
    The building of the Monnow Bridge (about 1240)
    The reign of James I (1603-1625)
    The Battle of Agincourt (1415)
    The building of Castle House (1673)
    The death of Nelson (1805)
    The Civil War (1642-1646)

▲ **2.** Choose one of the events on the list. Find out about it. Tape a short talk about it.

▲ **3.** Look at a 1p piece. On one side is a portcullis. Draw a picture of a portcullis. How was is used?

▲ **4.** Monmouth School is still run by the Haberdasher's Company. This company is one of the ancient guilds of the City of London. Find out what a guild was in the Middle Ages. Was it like a trade union today?

▲ **5.** Look at the time chart at the back of this book. Some of the events in the list are already on it. Where would you put the others?

5. Family history

In history books and on television we usually only learn about the history of great and powerful families, for example, the Royal Family.

However, every family has its own history. We can study our own families, and discover how great events in world history affected them. Most families still have souvenirs and photographs which tell us a great deal about their life in the past.

A class in a school in Lincolnshire decided to look at family history. They asked their parents and grandparents to show them old photographs of the family.

Many of the photographs were of weddings and babies. This did not seem very interesting at first. However, the children asked who the people were, how they were related, when they were born, married and had died. In this way, they began to build stories of life since 1900.

Look at the photographs. They show different generations of the family of one of the girls in the class.

Great grandparents
William b. 1880 d. 1976
Lilias b. 1881 d. 1947
married 1904

The four generations at my brother's christening in 1973

Great grandparents

George b. 1860 d. 1933
Jane b. 1861 d. 1944
married 1880

Grandparents

George b. 1905
May b. 1905
married 1934

Parents

Helen b. 1936
Neil b. 1929
married 1960

Her father's parents were dead. So she decided to study her mother's family because she could get more information about them. Her grandparents told her when their parents had been born, the work they did, and when they died. She listed this information under the photographs.

Look at the photographs and answer these questions.

● **A.** Which great-grandfather was born first?
● **B.** Which grandparent lived the longest?
● **C.** How can you tell that the photographs of the two sets of great-grandparents were taken at about the same time in the century?
● **D.** Look at the christening photograph. Name as many of the people as you can.

▲ **1.** If you can, find photographs of different generations of your family (or another family, if you prefer). Arrange them in a chart and put the dates of each person's birth, death and marriage underneath. If you have no photographs, write the names on a chart and put the information underneath. Use the photographs on this page to help you.

When she had finished the chart, she asked more questions about the jobs of the people shown in the photographs, and where they had been born.

Her grandparents showed other souvenirs and mementos which they had kept. They were able to tell her many interesting things about their parents. Here are some of the notes which she wrote out for the others in the class to read:

Great-grandfather George

1. Great Grandfather George was born in Knaresborough in Yorkshire. His wife, Jane, was born on a farm a few miles away.

2. When he lived in Knaresborough he drove visitors to Studley Royal Park in a horse-drawn carriage called a gig.

3. He played a musical instrument called a bombardon. This was a brass instrument which played low notes.

4. When they were married, they moved to Lincolnshire because George was given a job in a works which had a brass band (like the one in the photograph opposite).

5. He soon started his own sweet-making works. He made boiled sweets and was very good at making humbugs. He also made cough sweets. The label on the sweet jars had his photograph on it. There is a jar of humbugs with the family label on it in a museum in Lincoln today. Grandfather has the bank book for the account that was opened when the firm began. One son went

Knaresborough, where Great-grandfather George was born.

to Liverpool to work at the Everton toffee factory.

● **A.** What kind of carriage was a gig? You should find the answer in a dictionary.
● **B.** Name three other instruments in a brass band. The photograph may help.
● **C.** What kind of sweet is a humbug? Does it have another name?

▲ **1.** Find Knaresborough in an atlas. Then find Lincoln. About how far did George have to travel when he changed jobs?

Great-grandfather William

1. Great grandfather William was born in a little town in Lincolnshire. He started working on a farm as a boy. When he married, he was in charge of the teams of horses that worked on the farm.

2. His wife Lilias, was a true Cockney because she was born within the sound of Bow Bells in London. She was sent out to service (became a maid). The family she worked for took her to Lincolnshire where she met William.

3. When he got married in 1904, the farmer he worked for refused to raise his pay. So on the next Lady Day he walked to Lincoln to the hiring fair. He stood in a line along the street with other farmworkers who were looking for jobs. William found a new job with an extra one guinea a year pay. He stayed in his new job for many years.

● **D.** Why did farms in the past need large teams of horses?
● **E.** Look back at page 2 and find out what "Bow Bells" means.

▲ **2.** How would Lilias feel about leaving her family to go into service? Tape sentences describing her feelings.

4. Although William loved horses he left farming. This was because wages were very low, and he had to work very long hours. He had to have the horse teams ready by the time the other farmworkers came to work. After the others had finished for the day, William had to stay behind to make sure that the horses had been fed and groomed, and that the harness had been cleaned. So he took a job in an engineering works in a town just before the start of World War 1.

▲ **1.** You are William. You have just decided that you must give up your job working with horses. What are your feelings? Tape or write what you tell your wife Lilias. You may like to do this with a friend – one of you can be William, the other Lilias.

▲ **2.** Do you think William was right to change his job? Write down your reasons.

Grandfather

1. He kept the family firm going until he retired and sold it.

2. During World War 2 he was a member of the Air Raid Precaution service (ARP). Men in the ARP were called Wardens. They wore dark blue uniforms and carried whistles. They told people what to do during air raids.

3. He drove some of the earliest types of delivery vans when he worked for his father.

● **A.** What were air raids? Was the work of the ARP wardens dangerous?

● **B.** Look at the picture of the van. How can you tell it is old?

Grandmother

1. When Grandmother left school, she decided to become a teacher. In those days, there was no need to go to college to train. Instead she became a "pupil teacher" — a kind of apprentice. She worked in a local school and was supervised by the headmistress.

Pupil teachers worked hard. Every term the headmistress wrote a report on her work. It was just like the school report you have today. The reports were also checked by school inspectors. After two years of pupil teaching, she was able to look for a job in a local primary school.

2. In those days women teachers were not allowed to keep their jobs when they married. So Grandmother had to give up teaching when she married Grandfather.

3. After World War 2, Grandmother returned to teaching for a few years. She taught in a village school. She had some American children in her class. Their fathers were Air Force officers at the nearby airfield.

● C. Why was Grandmother called a pupil teacher?
● D. What was the work of the school inspector? (Ask your teacher.)

Pupil Teacher's Centre Report.

● E. Why do you think an inspector checked the report of the headmistress?
● F. Do you think it right that women had to give up teaching when they married? Give your reasons.
● G. Why were American forces stationed in Britain after the end of World War 2?

▲ 3. You have been finding out about a family. Choose two of the people in it. Write down interesting points about them.

Family trees

When you have found out about the different generations in your family, you can make a "family tree". This is like the generation chart the girl made, but it does not usually include photographs. It also shows more than one branch of the family.

● **A.** Why do you think it is called a "family tree"?

People who find information about family history are called genealogists. One boy in the class had an uncle who was very keen on genealogy. He had traced his family back to 1724. The earliest member of the family he had found was a farmer in Essex.

Opposite is the family tree of William Henry Fox Talbot, who started modern photography in Britain. He lived in Lacock Abbey in Wiltshire. His family owned the abbey from the reign of King Henry VIII (1509-1547) until 1944. The first photographs he took were of his home.

● **B.** How can you tell from the chart that William Henry Fox Talbot was a member of Parliament?
● **C.** How many children did he have?

The Fox Talbot family tree

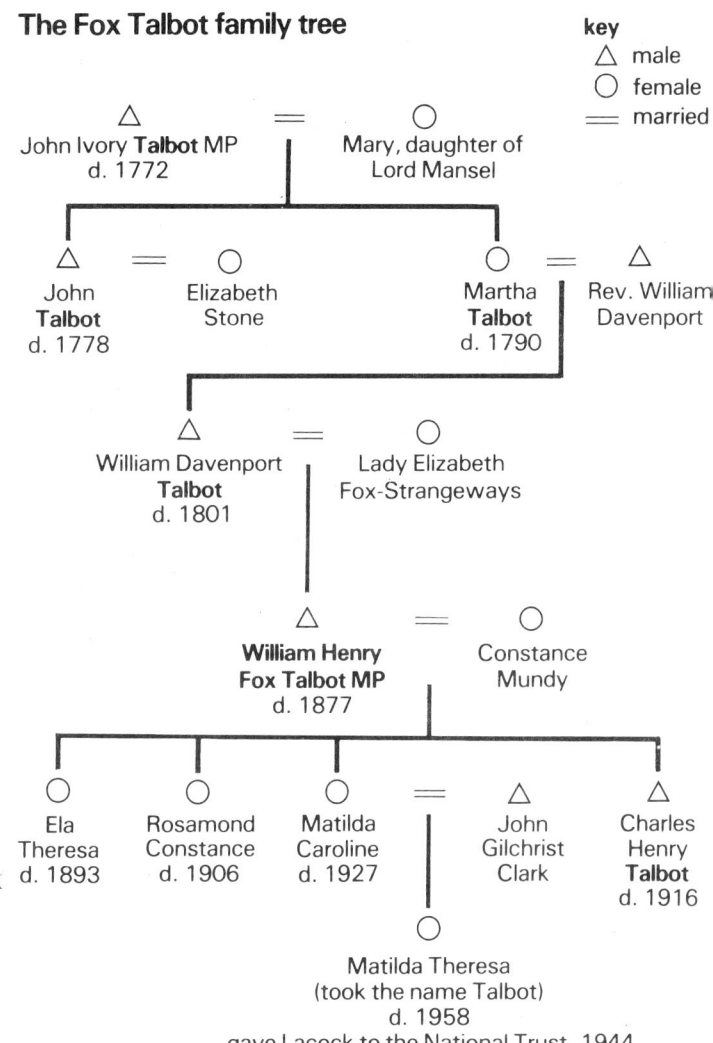

key
△ male
○ female
= married

John Ivory **Talbot** MP d. 1772 = Mary, daughter of Lord Mansel

John **Talbot** d. 1778 = Elizabeth Stone

Martha **Talbot** d. 1790 = Rev. William Davenport

William Davenport **Talbot** d. 1801 = Lady Elizabeth Fox-Strangeways

William Henry Fox Talbot MP d. 1877 = Constance Mundy

Ela Theresa d. 1893
Rosamond Constance d. 1906
Matilda Caroline d. 1927
John Gilchrist Clark
Charles Henry **Talbot** d. 1916

Matilda Theresa (took the name Talbot) d. 1958
gave Lacock to the National Trust, 1944

● **D.** His name might have been Davenport. Why?
● **E.** From whom did he get the name "Fox"?
● **F.** For how many years did the family own the abbey?

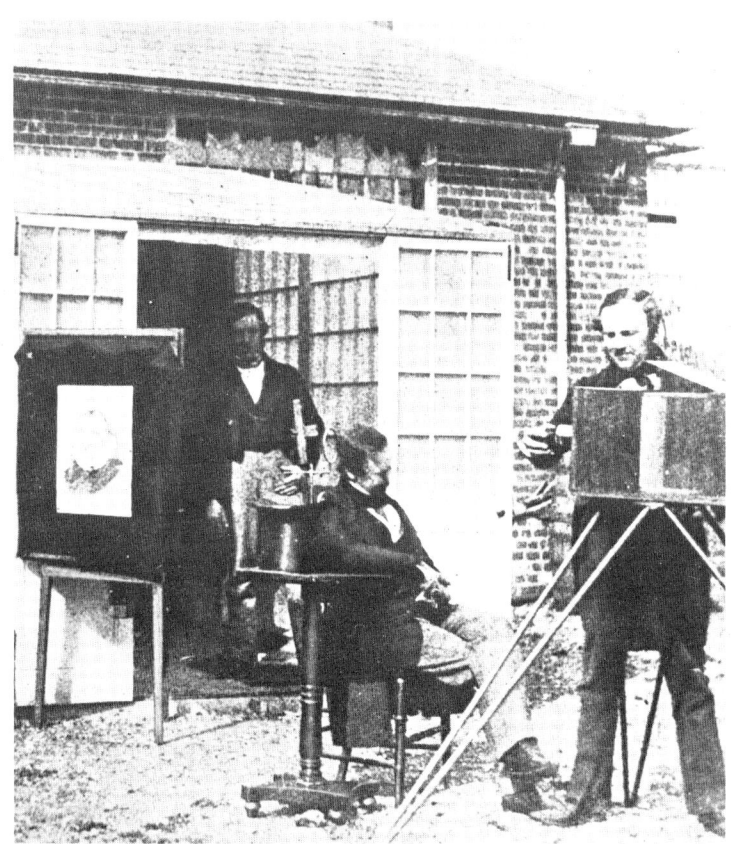

Some of William Henry Fox Talbot's friends at his home.

Above you can see a photograph taken by William Henry Fox Talbot. You can also see one of the cameras he used.

If you live in or near to Wiltshire you may have the chance to visit Lacock and to see some of Fox Talbot's early cameras.

▲ 1. Talbot's grand-daughter, Matilda, gave Lacock Abbey to the National Trust in 1944. Find out what the National Trust is. Why do people leave houses and land to it?

▲ 2. Find out which is the nearest National Trust property to your home.

▲ 3. Use the information you have collected so far to draw a family tree like the Fox Talbot tree.

31

6. Looking at newspapers

R.A.F. smash Goering's Sunday raids on London by 400 planes

175 SHOT DOWN

The newspaper headline above was printed in 1940. British RAF aeroplanes were fighting German planes in the Battle of Britain. This headline reports the time when the RAF planes started to win. The German Luftwaffe (air force) lost many planes in raids on London. The Germans could not invade Britain because they could not defeat the RAF.

On the same page, there was a story of how the lawns of Buckingham Palace had caught fire from the bombs. The newspaper said it was the third attempt to kill the King and Queen.

- **A.** Why would the Germans want to kill the King and Queen?
- **B.** The picture opposite shows a wedding in 1947. Who are the couple getting married?
- **C.** Choose the right word from the brackets. The bride in the photograph is the (daughter, sister, mother) of the King mentioned in the newspaper article.

- **D.** What was the name of the King in World War 2?

National newspapers like the *Daily Express* report news from our own country and other countries. All the great events in history in the last two hundred years have been reported by newspapers.

▲ **1.** Make a collection of newspaper headlines that will be interesting in 20 years time.

This children's fête was held in Hyde Park in 1887. It celebrated the jubilee of Queen Victoria. She had been Queen for 50 years.

In the early days of newspapers, it was not possible to print photographs as we do today. Artists drew pictures of the main events and these were printed.

The Graphic was a famous London newspaper. Above is *The Graphic's* picture of a schoolchildren's fête in Hyde Park on June 22nd, 1887.

Look at the picture and caption. Answer these questions:

- **E.** What did the fête celebrate?
- **F.** What does the picture in the right-hand corner show?
- **G.** It was a very fine day, so what were the ladies carrying?

Thirty thousand children from all the schools in London were invited to the fête. Each child was given a paper bag full of food. They had meat pies, pieces of cake, buns and an orange. There were tents around the park in which they could get lemonade, ginger beer and milk.

There were also entertainments, such as punch and judy shows, performing dogs and lucky dips.

Each child received a medal and presents. A thousand skipping ropes, 10 000 balloons and 42 000 toys were given away.

▲ **2.** Imagine you were at the fête. Write or tape a story about what you did there.

33

CENTENARY NEWS EDITION

FRIDAY, MAY 13th, 1955

1855 Hundred Years of Newspaper History 1955

The pupils in one class were asked to go to the town library in their own time and look at the copies of old local newspapers. Their teacher asked them to find things that especially interested them. Back in class, they discussed what they had found. They made a list of the main types of news. Here is their list:

sport
entertainments
events such as dances
changes in the town
advertisements for shops
market news
weather
industry and jobs
national news that
   affected the town

The children found some important pieces of local history in the old newspapers.

Some of the class talked about their work in school when they went home. One girl's parents gave her a copy of the centenary edition of a local paper published in the Midlands. The paper was printed in 1955. It was a little torn and the outside pages had turned yellow, but there was a lot of very interesting information printed in it.

● **A.** What do we mean by a "centenary" edition?
● **B.** Where are the Midlands?
● **C.** Look at an atlas and name three important cities in the Midlands.

▲ **1.** Ask your science teacher why old newspapers turn yellow. Write out the answers you get.
▲ **2.** Look at this week's edition of your own local newspaper. If your school still exists after 50 years, what stories do you think would interest the pupils? Why?

The class thought that page 9 of the centenary edition was the most interesting part. The page had the title "100 years of headlines". Underneath were listed some of the headline news that had been on the front page during the previous 100 years.

The class made a chart of the most interesting ones. Here is their chart.

One hundred years of news

May, 1855	First edition of the "Gainsborough News"
July, 1857	First passenger train from the town to Doncaster
April, 1864	A ship collided with a two ton whale in the River Trent
March, 1869	Town meeting to raise £2000 to buy the toll bridge over the river for the town
September, 1873 . .	Gainsborough Trinity F.C. formed
January, 1879	Cricket match played on ice-covered Lea Marshes
January, 1884	King's Theatre burned down
December, 1897 . . .	First car driven over toll bridge

Look at the chart and answer these questions:

- **D.** How many of the headlines are about the weather?
- **E.** Which is the most unusual headline?
- **F.** How many of the headlines listed were linked with sport?
- **G.** In 1869 the town did not manage to buy the toll bridge, and therefore did not make it free of charge. How do you know this? (Look at December, 1897.)
- **H.** The cartoon shows one of the events in the list. What date did it happen?

You will also find interesting historical information in the Sunday newspaper magazines. In 1975 it was 30 years since the end of World War 2 in Europe. The day when the war finished is called V.E. Day. Here is some information about the war. It was published in the *Observer Magazine*, May 4th, 1975.

Sheila Hancock, the actress, was a small girl in 1945. She remembers a street party on V.E. day.

"People put up trestle tables in the street. We had orange and lemon drinks and junket, which seemed to be the staple diet at parties. In the evening the grown-ups lit bonfires. I was allowed to stay up really late and dance.

We climbed a hill and looked at the bonfires burning all over London."

● **A.** What is a "staple diet"?
● **B.** Junket is a sort of creamy pudding. What is the "staple diet" at parties today?
● **C.** Why have there been changes?

Another lady who had been in the A.T.S. (the women's army), was in London on V.E. day. She went to Piccadilly Circus.

"I shinned up a lamp post to get a better view.
I later decided to wend my way up the Mall, and ended up in front of Buckingham Palace where the crowds were really frightening. The King and Queen were out on the balcony. I stayed there for hours shouting and cheering my head off."

● **D.** Why do you think newspapers and magazines think that war anniversaries are important news items?

▲ **1.** Draw a picture showing what V.E. Day was like.

36

In 1979 you may remember there were many newspaper articles and television programmes about World War 2. This was because it was the 40th anniversary of the start of that war. Here are some other anniversaries which may make headlines in the 1980s.

1981	300th anniversary of the founding of Pennsylvania by William Penn
1982	700th anniversary of the completion of the conquest of Wales by Edward I
1983	150th anniversary of the abolition of slavery in the British Empire
	25th anniversary of the founding of the European Economic Community (the Common Market)
1984	50th anniversary of the death of Madame Curie
1985	500th annniversary of the Battle of Bosworth which brought the Tudors to the throne
	500th anniversary of the founding of the Yeomen of the Guard
1986	50th anniversary of the abdication of Edward VIII
	25th anniversary of man's first flight in space
1987	100th anniversary of Queen Victoria's Jubilee

● **E.** Which is the earliest event on the list?
● **F.** How many of the events listed had nothing to do with this country?
● **G.** What does the word 'abdication' mean?
● **H.** What happened in 1282?
● **I.** What happened in 1961?

● **K.** This picture is connected with one of the events on the list. Which one?

▲ **2.** Choose one of the events in the list. Draw a picture which could be used as the design for a stamp printed in memory of the event.
▲ **3.** Use local newspapers to make a list of the anniversaries for your district in the 1980s.

7. Using maps and charts in history

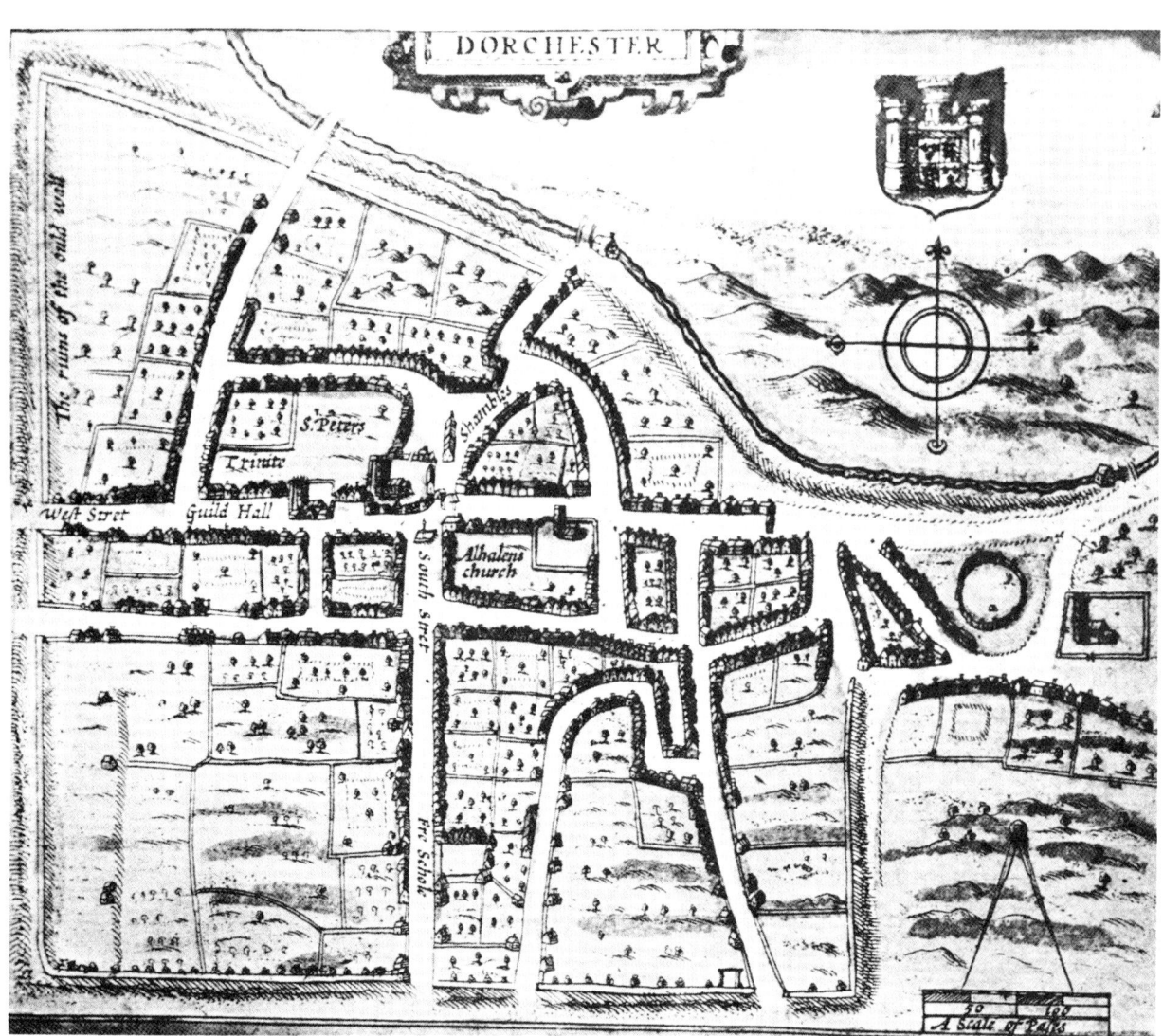

Historians do much of their practical work in libraries where they study documents. Old maps are very useful documents. Historical maps may help historians to work out what a town was like in the past and the way in which it has grown to its present size. Some maps of country areas may show what was grown in the fields, who owned the land, and who lived in houses shown on the map.

Opposite is a copy of an old map of Dorchester. It was drawn by a man named John Speed in 1610. Speed made an atlas of the counties of England and Wales. In the corner of the map of the county, he usually drew a plan of the county town.

● **A.** He drew this map of Dorchester in the corner of a county map. Which county was it?

From this map the historians can see what Dorchester was like in 1610. It had a very simple plan. The first town on the site had been built by the Romans and the plan had not changed much. If we look at the map of 1610 and a map of modern Dorchester it is easy to see how the town has grown and changed.

▲ **1.** Make a list of the names of the streets shown on the map.

The high street of Dorchester today.

● **B.** How many churches can you find?
● **C.** Why do you think there is a pair of compasses over the scale?
● **D.** Was Dorchester a large town? Give reasons for your answer.
● **E.** What did the word 'shambles' mean in the past? What does it mean today?
● **F.** Why do you think John Speed put coats of arms on his maps?
● **G.** Why did cartographers decorate maps?

▲ **2.** Look at the picture of modern Dorchester. Write down the things that might have been there at the time the map was drawn. Write down the things that were not there.

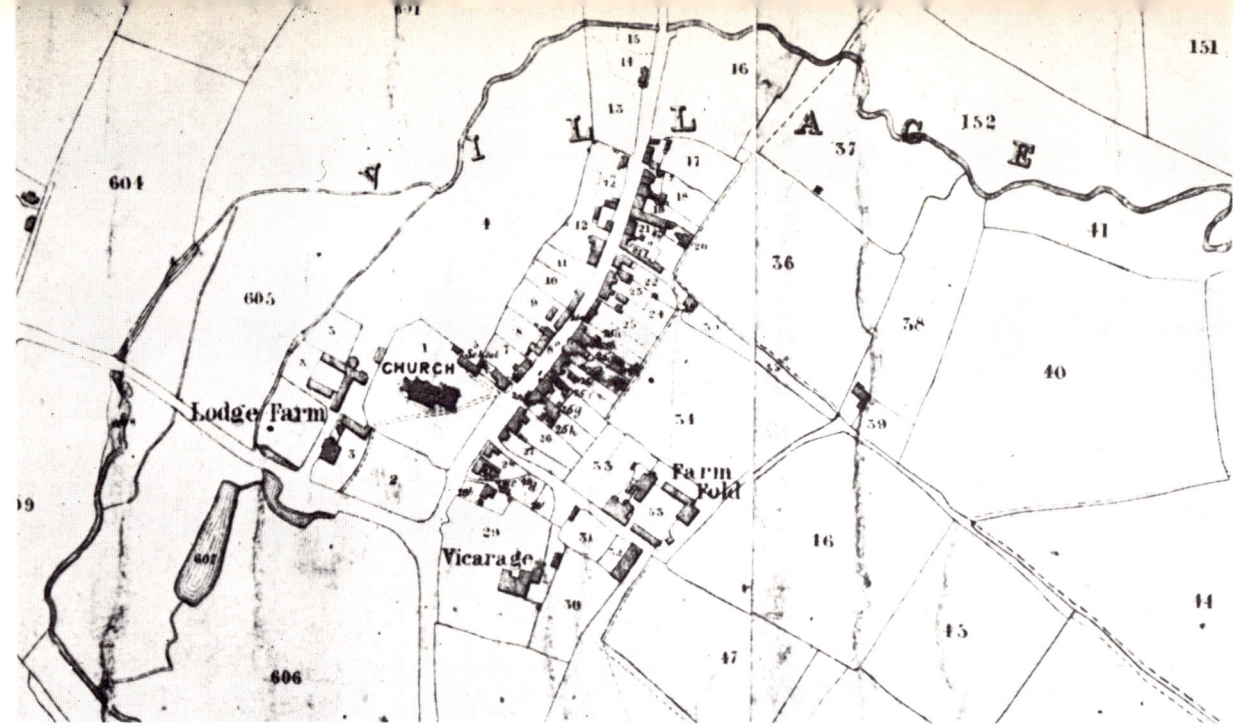

Tithe plans

Above, you can see part of a map of a village in Worcestershire in 1840. It is called Chaddesley Corbett. The buildings in the village and the fields are numbered.

Thousands of maps like this were made about 150 years ago. They were maps of the parishes in England and Wales. They are called tithe plans. A tithe was a tax paid to the church. It was about one-tenth of what a farm grew or a tenth of the rent of a house. The tithe might be paid in money or in crops or animals. Remember the tithe barn at Bredon on page 6. It was built to hold the crops paid as tithes.

In 1836 Parliament decided that all tithes should be paid in money. Surveyors were sent all over the country to make maps of the parishes, and to decide how much tithe the landowners had to pay. About 12 000 maps were made, and they still exist.

● **A.** Why was it better to pay tithes in money?
● **B.** Why were landowners expected to pay a tithe to the church?

The tithe maps are especially important to historians. They can use the information on the maps to get a very full picture of what the village was like at the time the map was made.

The Talbot Inn in Chaddesley Corbett. This photograph was taken in 1979.

The numbers on the map match up with a list which is called the "schedule". The schedule for Chadesley Corbett tells us, for example, that number 12 on the map belonged to the corporation of the City of Warwick. It is listed as a house with a garden and Thomas Bate lived in it. Here are some others.

No.	Owner	Tenant	What it was
2	Sir Charles Throckmorton	James Blakeway	Orchard
89	Corporation of Warwick	Samuel Potter	Shop
25	Eliza Williams	Mary Jackson	Talbot Inn yard and garden

Fields were also numbered. So we know that in 1840 Elizabeth Bate owned field 157. We also know that it was called Barn Close, and that it was used for growing crops. Elizabeth had to pay a tithe of 17/6d (seventeen shillings and six old pence) a year on it.

● C. What is 17/6d in today's money?
● D. What does the word "schedule" mean? (use a dictionary)
● E. Look at the photograph of the Talbot. Do you think it is the same building as the one which was there in 1840?

▲ 1. You are a farmer in 1840. Your harvest was very poor. Write a letter to the vicar explaining why you can't pay your tithes.

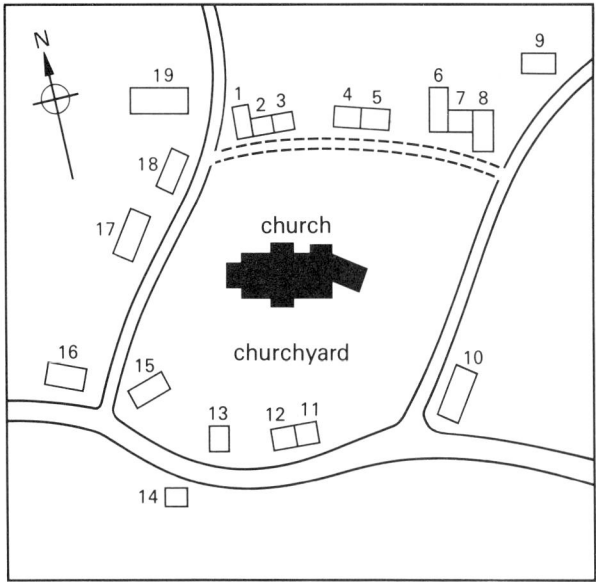

A class decided to make its own map of historical places near their school. They decided to look at the buildings around the church. They drew a map showing the church and the buildings, then they gave each building a number (just like the buildings on the tithe plan).

They decided to make a survey of the buildings they had put on the map. They wanted to look at two things:
(a) the age of the buildings
(b) the materials used to build them

First they decided on three age groups in which they could put the buildings. These were:

(a) recent (up to 20 years old)
(b) fairly old (between 20 and 100 years old)
(c) old (more than 100 years old)

They wanted to find out if different materials were used to make the buildings in each of these three periods. To help them they made a key like this.

ROOF		WALLS	
Materials	Symbol	Materials	Symbol
Slate	S	Stone	ST
thatch	T H	brick	B
tiles	T	flint	F
other Materials	O	wood	W
		brick and timber	BT
		tile hung	T
		other Materials	O

Then they drew up a survey sheet. Look at the copy opposite.

- **A.** In what way are all the buildings alike?
- **B.** When were most of the houses built?
- **C.** Were all the old houses built of the same materials?
- **D.** The recently built houses were made of the same materials as the older ones. Why is this so?

42

Building		Age	Building materials	
no.	type		roof	walls
1	house	f. old	T	B
2	house	f. old	T	BT
3	house	f. old	T	BT
4	house	f. old	T	B
5	house	f. old	T	B
6	house	old	T	T
7	house	old	T	BT
8	house	old	T	B
9	house	f. old	T	BT
10	vicarage	old	T	B
11	house	f. old	T	BT
12	house	f. old	T	BT
13	house	f. old	T	BT
14	house	f. old	T	BT
15	house	old	T	BT
16	house	f. old	T	T
17	house	recent	T	BT
18	house	recent	T	BT
19	old school	old	T	F

▲ 1. Trace the map opposite. Use the survey sheet to find out which age group each building on the map is in.

Use a different colour for each age group.

Colour the old buildings red. Colour the fairly old buildings blue, and the recent buildings green.

Add a key to your map, so that people can see what the colours mean.

▲ 2. Trace the map again. This time use the survey sheet to find out what the walls of each building are made of.

Choose colours to stand for each building material — for example, red for wood. Colour the map.
Add a key.

● E. Look at your two maps. What can you find out by comparing them?

▲ 3. For each of the buildings on the map make a symbol, a square for a house, for example.

Choose a colour to represent each building material, and colour each symbol.

Make a chart to show the things you have found out.

8. Collecting historical evidence

People make objects and buildings which are left behind when the people die. The things made by people who lived in the past are now buried in the ground or under water. Archaeologists are people who uncover these things. They also study them to find out how people lived in the past. They are finding evidence.

It is not often than an archaeologist is lucky enough to make as exciting a discovery as the one opposite. The photograph shows the uncovering of a Saxon cemetery in Sussex.

The things archaeologists find are called artifacts. The archaeologist is able to 'read' the past by finding out what they are, how old they are and putting them in the right order.

You do not need to be a professional archaeologist to find artifacts which help you understand the past. The artifacts do not need to be very old.

● **A.** Why do some people prefer to do history by uncovering things, rather than learning from books?

● **B.** What are the advantages of digging for yourself?

● **C.** How can you tell that the picture shows a cemetery (burial ground)?

The Glory of a Lion is his Mane.

One Saturday morning a group of children found some old uniform buttons and an army cap on a market stall. They found they could buy these objects cheaply. So they decided to make a collection of World War 1 artifacts.

They began to look around other stalls and shops. They found medals, framed photographs, and bits of uniform. They also found a World War 1 German helmet. In some shops they found old postcards. Some of these postcards came from France. In the war, soldiers had sent them to their families.

Some cards had been used in this country. They were patriotic cards. They had slogans and pictures of war leaders.

Above is one of the patriotic cards. Look at the lion's mane carefully.

● **D.** What does "patriotic" mean?
● **E.** Why do people send patriotic cards in time of war?
● **F.** Why did many of the cards come from France?

▲ **1.** Write out in your own words what you think the card above means.

▲ **2.** Ask permission to look around an antique shop or a market junk stall. Make a list of World War 1 artifacts. If possible draw some of them. In class, make a chart with your drawings and try to find out something about the artifacts. Write it on the chart.

45

One of the books contained the photograph on the left. It shows four women air mechanics working on an R.A.F. plane during World War 1. The plane was an Avro biplane.

- **A.** How can you tell that it was an R.A.F. plane?
- **B.** What was a biplane?
- **C.** Why do you think so many people were working on a single plane?

In class on Monday, the children passed one of the uniform buttons around.

"How do you know it's off a man's uniform and not off a woman's?" asked one of the girls.

"Only men fought in World War 1" answered one of the boys.

An argument started. It was still going on when the teacher walked into the classroom. The next day, she brought some books with her to show the class. The books showed what women did in World War 1 and World War 2.

Some of the girls liked the photographs the teacher had shown them. They decided to do a project called "Women at War". They found information in books in the school library and in the local library.

They found that in World War 1 women had served their country in three main ways:

1. by taking over all kinds of work as the men went off to fight (for example, in factories).
2. by working as nurses and ambulance drivers in this country and abroad. They were needed to look after wounded soldiers.
3. late in the war by joining the new women's branches of the three main services — the navy, army and air force.

During World War 1, many thousands of women went to France and Belgium to help with the wounded. The women who worked in hospitals and camps behind the front line were in danger. The photograph below shows a woman ambulance driver being given a medal for bravery.

During World War 2 many women were ordered by the government to join the armed forces — we say they were conscripted. From December 1941 all unmarried women between the ages of 20 and 30 could be called up (told to join). The most famous conscript was Princess Elizabeth (now the Queen), who joined the A.T.S.

● **D.** What was a conscript?
● **E.** Why were women needed in the services?

When the girls discovered what women did, they asked their grandmothers if they had been in the forces. One of the girls brought a photograph to school. It showed her grandmother as an Aircraftwoman.

▲ **1.** Talk to people who remember World War 2 to get some idea of what it was like. Then *either* imagine you have been called up for service *or* imagine someone in your family has been called up. Make a tape describing how you feel.

▲ **2.** Make a class collection of photographs of people during the war. You can use photographs from magazines too. Make a chart and tape sentences to describe the photographs.

This woman ambulance driver in World War 1 is receiving a medal for bravery.

The two pictures above show scenes from World War 1. The first picture is an advertisement. The second is a photograph of soldiers at the front (where the war was fought).

- **A.** What does the second picture show?
- **B.** Look at the advertisement. What does it make World War 1 seem like?
- **C.** Look at the photograph. What does World War 1 seem like?

- **D.** Which gives a truer picture, the photograph or the advertisement. Why?
- **E.** Why does the advertisement show war in this way?

Both the advertisement and the photograph are pieces of historical evidence. They each tell us something different about World War 1. We can learn more by comparing them than by looking at each of them separately.

So, when we collect historical evidence, it is important to look at all the pieces together. Sometimes, the evidence may seem to tell us opposite things (like these pictures do). We have to work out what this means. Then we can build up a true picture of how things were in the past.